Anita
Kuny.

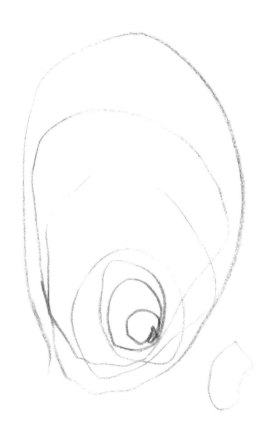

MUSIC MAKER

Robina Beckles Willson

Illustrated by Gunvor Edwards

VIKING KESTREL

VIKING KESTREL
Penguin Books Ltd, Harmondsworth, Middlesex, England
Viking Penguin Inc., 40 West 23rd Street, New York, New York 10010, U.S.A.
Penguin Books Australia Ltd, Ringwood, Victoria, Australia
Penguin Books Canada Ltd, 2801 John Street, Markham, Ontario, Canada L3R 1B4
Penguin Books (N.Z.) Ltd, 182–190 Wairau Road, Auckland 10, New Zealand

First published 1986

Text copyright © Robina Beckles Willson, 1986
Illustrations copyright © Gunvor Edwards, 1986

British Library Cataloguing in Publication Data

Beckles-Willson, Robina
    Music maker.
    1. Music—Juvenile literature
    I. Title
    780   ML3930.A2

    ISBN 0-670-80527-0

Photoset by Rowland Phototypesetting Ltd,
Bury St Edmunds, Suffolk
Printed in Great Britain by
Butler & Tanner Ltd, Frome, Somerset

With love to Rachel,
whose music making
gives me so much pleasure

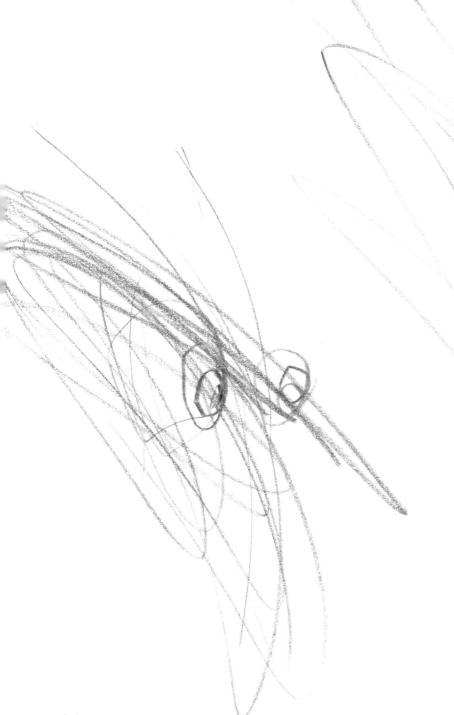

Contents

Acknowledgements

Many people have given me help in the preparation of this book, but in particular I should like to thank: Mark and Rachel Beckles Willson; Catherine Burchill, who typed the manuscript with infinite patience; Lucy Floyer; Anna Furze, Alexander Macpherson and the boys and girls at Bishop Kirk Middle School, Oxford; the Lady Eleanor Holles School Junior Department, Hampton; Glenda Parkinson, who wrote the music for the mini-opera; Jenny Sutton and the Music Club at Saint Mary's Junior School, Twickenham. Jennie Walters has been an indefatigable editor.

I have been inspired by the music making of many children, especially at the Richmond upon Thames Music Festival; concerts at the Lady Eleanor Holles School, and at Chase Bridge Junior School, Whitton; and the holiday courses and concerts arranged by the Kingston Association for Music Education (Kame).

R. B. W.

Cover Notes

Paul Emerton, pictured on the cover, can make music or noises with these: a kazoo and a harmonica on a bracket, on which is also tied a string of foil milk-bottle tops; and, dangling from a frame made by a plastic-covered coat-hanger: a cymbal, a hand bell, a bongo, a triangle, jingles on a stick, a tambourine and a chain. He is holding jingle bells and is wearing bells sewn on to elastic, and a recorder.

Danielle Emerton has a finger cymbal for an ear-ring, jingle bells sewn on to her beret and bracelets and anklets of jingle bells too, with larger bells on a string round her waist. She is blowing a rubber trumpet and has a cymbal and saucepan lid to beat, and a recorder to blow as well.

Paul and Danielle's clothes were kindly loaned by Benetton.

1

How You Make Sounds

You yourself are a musical instrument. First, you are a wind instrument, because your voice can sing. You can make tunes. These sounds are made by vocal cords, which vibrate inside a voice box, in your throat. The air is sent out from the lungs to set your voice singing.

Look in the mirror and sing these sounds: 'ah-eye-eee-ooh-oh.' Do it slowly, so that you can notice how your mouth changes shape and your tongue changes position inside your mouth.

Ah   Eye   Eeh   Ooh   Oh

If you sing with your mouth shut, the humming sound escapes as the air in the spaces inside your mouth, nose and neck is vibrating, or reverberating. If you sing the sounds holding your nose tightly, you will notice at once that the sound changes when the nose is blocked. Singers find colds particularly troublesome, and you can hear why. Their voices change.

Making noises

Perhaps a less musical sound is to open your mouth and make 'glug' sounds in the back of your throat. You can also try a gargling sound with your voice by holding some water in your mouth, tipping your head back a little, then saying 'ah', which makes the water gurgle.

Now shut your mouth and blow out your cheeks as far as you can. Tap them with your first (index) finger, and you hear a little popping sound. If you open your mouth the sound goes higher.

Sing 'ah' and move your index finger up and down quickly between your lips. You'll hear a warbling, jungly sort of sound. Sing 'ah' again, and tap the top of your chest, so that the sound vibrates.

You can make a more musical sound by whistling. Tunes whistled sound good in the open air, and sometimes birds will answer you, which is rather flattering, as if they think you do it well, like one of them.

You can keep yourself company by whistling. It is less easy to keep in time and tune with a record or the radio. Ordinary whistling is with pursed lips pushed forward, pressing the air out. Another version is to whistle through the teeth, and any gaps between them, with the mouth slightly open in a smiling position. This sound is thinner and more breathy. Try it out.

To gain attention, there is a piercing whistle with fingers in your mouth. Put the index and middle fingers together upright, with the thumb alongside, and the other two fingers curled back. Next put your hands together so that the baby fingers are touching. Curl your tongue upwards a little. Now put the two pairs of fingers into your mouth so that they touch your tongue. Sometimes the tips of the finger pairs will touch each other in your mouth. Close your mouth round the fingers, leaving a gap in the middle.

Then blow very gently, taking care to keep the gap open as you move your lips. It is not easy, but keep trying, and in the end you will get a note.

Finger whistling

With your musical mouth you can also make popping noises and clicks like horses' hooves by curling up your tongue and tapping it up sharply on the roof of your mouth. If you hold your tongue in that position, and then move it slightly, you'll discover even stranger sounds, which you may or may not think musical.

Still thinking of yourself as an instrument, you can make sounds with your hands. Tap with your fingernails or fingertips on a hard surface, like glass, metal, or wood, and notice the different sounds. Then push your thumb against your middle finger so firmly that it makes a loud click.

Clap with straight fingers on your other fingers or on your palm. If you clap with both hands flat, then hollow them by curving them, the second sound will be deeper. Another noise can be made by clapping your knees, thighs or sides, and you will hear what a difference wearing clothes makes to the sound.

Hand clapping, with cupped and flat hands

If you want your feet to make sounds you can try stamping, or, for a more muddled noise, shuffling them around on the floor. They can shush through autumn leaves or rattle among pebbles or shingle.

You can be a one-man-band

The idea of being an instrument can be carried out in a way which clowns and street musicians have often used, to make people laugh and enjoy a mixture of musical and not so musical sounds. The more instruments a clown can handle as he walks along, the better band he is. In a procession he is so bedecked with instruments that he sounds like a whole band.

As you work out your instruments you need to consider what will sound if moved about. It must be fastened to you in such a way that it is free to vibrate as you move, or be set in vibration, for example by drumsticks. Also, it is worth trying to produce sounds which contrast with each other. So think of noises made by blowing, shaking, banging and rattling, if you can.

Head
Starting with your head, you can make a hat hung with rustles of twisted silver paper streamers, and strings of threaded milk-bottle tops. Or you could sew jingles to a cap or beret.

Ears
Small cymbals can be ear-rings, and so can threaded bells.

Mouth

Blow a harmonica, which can be on a wire bracket to free your hands. Or blow a whistle, a recorder or a kazoo.

Neck

Hang jangling chains or a large open tambourine round your neck. You can also use plastic-coated wire to rig up a support frame for various contraptions. It can hold a tray with a xylophone or a drum to beat. A tinkling bell can dangle on a string from the frame.

Under the arm

A rubber hooter can be tied to your upper arm so that you squeeze the rubber bulb when you press your arm to your side.

Waist

At waist level, you can have a drum or two to beat. A drum is a good contrast with a recorder, and the two produce the same sort of sound as a drum and fife band.

One drum could be a large plastic paint container. Another drum could be made from a plastic flower pot covered with tightly stretched leather or plastic (see page 33). A contrasting drum sound could be made by tapping the membrane or head of a tambourine.

From your belt, saucepan lids, saucepans and a triangle or other metal object could hang down and clash together when you move.

Elbows and wrists

Jingles or small bells can be tied to elbows or wrists.

Instruments for a one-man band: hats with milk bottle top streamers and small bells, bell ear-rings; a harmonica on a support, drums, a neck chain, a tray holding a xylophone, saucepans hanging from a belt; a rubber hooter under the arm; bells and beaters around the wrist; foil plates, cymbals, tins and lids around the knees; bells and rattles around ankles and feet.

Hands

You may be holding beaters or a blowing instrument, but you can tie beaters on to your wrists on strings, to free your hands for various jobs. One can be shaking a rattle of some kind.

Knees

On the insides of your knees, you can tie things to clash against each other as you walk along. Try foil plates, cymbals, saucepan lids, or tobacco tins filled with rattling dried peas. String can be fastened on to the tins with sticky tape.

Ankles

Tie jingles or little bells round your ankles, or a rattle on the outside of your leg.

*　　*　　*

Be inventive. Try out your own ideas, gathering together what you can. Do make sure that everything is secure. If your collection falls to pieces it spoils the marvellous effect of one person producing so many sounds at the same time. When you feel ready, practise marching along and work out how to 'sound' every piece of your band. Make up a sort of pattern, so that you can blow, beat, rattle and clash, but not always all together. If you move in a little dance step it will make your progress as a one-man-band funnier to watch and to hear.

Even one person with four or five parts to his band can make a loud noise. If there are six or seven of you it is a tremendous din.

(See also the chapter on home-made instruments, pages 24–37.)

2
Vibrations

After all the noise of a one-man-band, you can try something more simple. Find a piece of elastic. Hold it at each end, stretched out. Then, without letting go, just pluck at the elastic with your right thumb. The vibration you cause makes the sound. If you stretch a long section it makes a deeper note than if you have a short length vibrating.

Prove it for yourself. Take a strong rubber band and stretch it round your left hand. Pluck at it with your right index finger, and you will notice that a different sound comes from the section across from the thumb to the smallest finger, and the short section between thumb and index finger. The sound will vary, not only according to how long your elastic is, but to how thick and how tightly stretched.

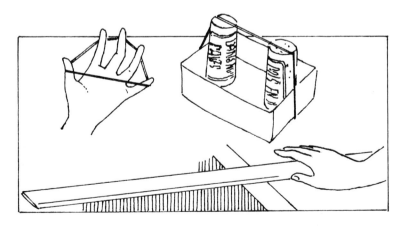

Elastic bands, ready for plucking, and a ruler, ready for twanging

These sounds soon fade away, as the elastic stops vibrating. If you stretch your elastic over an open box, like a large match box or a cut out cereal box, and then pluck, the sound does not fade so quickly. It is held inside the box, which has become a sound box, or resonator. You can also lift up the elastic over two corks or pieces of wood and stretch it tightly for plucking. This time the elastic string vibrates and echoes on the box. (See also pages 26–27.)

Place a long ruler with half its length on the table and lean your right hand on it to keep it firm. Then pluck at the section overhanging, and it will make a throbbing note, very satisfyingly.

To make a clear sound an object must be free to vibrate. For instance, try vibrating some bowls. You may be surprised by the lovely sounds hidden in your kitchen. Put out on the bare table a glass or pottery mixing bowl, a pudding basin and a soup or cereal bowl, whatever you can find. Tap the sides of each one with a wooden spoon, then a metal spoon. You'll notice that the metal spoon produces a sharper chime, and a good note, really like a bell. The sound fades slowly, but you can stop it instantly by touching the bowl with your left hand. That checks the vibration and acts as a damper.

Blowing

Blowing can set up vibrations which make sound too. This is often done by blowing against the opening of a container. Your breath sets the air inside the container vibrating, but you don't need to force air into it. The air is already inside, for you to set in motion. Your little puff of air is invisibly doing the playing. Once you start hunting you will discover that many objects sound a clear note if you blow against them gently, experimenting to find out which lip position works best.

Blow carefully across the top of a glass milk bottle, and it will sound a note. So will the top of a pen, a different noise altogether.

You probably know that you can blow a note if you cut a drinking straw into a wedge shape. Don't blow too hard. (See also page 29.) A more surprising way of making a musical tone is to blow through a triangular plastic slide binder. It sounds like a thin whistle. Hold the binder in your right hand, and rest it on the palm of your left hand.

Blow through the top. Try for different notes by squeezing the binder at different points.

Blowing across the top of a pen, and a drinking straw cut into a wedge, and through a plastic slide binder

Rubbing

Rubbing too can cause vibrations which produce sounds. If you can manage to stretch a string really tightly it will show this. Remember that metal or wire can cut if you are not careful with your fingers. A cheese-cutting wire which has little wooden handles at each end can be made taut by placing one foot carefully on a wooden handle, then holding the wire upwards from the floor. If you then rub the string with a wooden lolly stick it will make a sound.

You can also use nylon string, a plastic bottle, a cork, a small block of wood or box, and a stick or bamboo garden cane to make this kind of noise. You may need help, cutting a hole in the bottle, slicing the cork to wedge in the stick, and tying knots. But you can fiddle around to get the idea of the tight string vibrating, even if it's only by holding it on the table. Do what you can.

A CHEESE CUTTING WIRE

Another intriguing method is to make drinking glasses ring. Do ask permission first. Wine glasses work best. Hold a glass flat on the table with your left hand. Then rub round the top of the glass with a finger moistened with water. This needs steady pressure, and you may do it most easily with your middle finger. Persist, and your glass will ring out with a piercing sound, which some people find heavenly.

On a larger scale, you can 'disturb' the air waves out of doors. Give yourself plenty of room. Take a wooden ruler with a hole at one end, and a long strong nylon string, say about a metre and a half, tied to it. Be sure that no one is near to be clonked by it. If you are not very tall it is probably easiest to hold a section of the string dangling downwards, then circle the ruler on up to a metre of string either in front of you or over your head. When you get it going the noise from the whirling ruler will be a distant roaring. You have made a very simple version of the bull-roarer, which tribes used to imitate thunder and try and bring rain, by magic.

Amplification

You can work out for yourself how to increase or amplify the volume of sound you make. You will have seen the electric amplifiers used by pop groups to bump up the sound of their music.

In a modest way, you can do the same. Find some cardboard tube stiffeners, like those holding foil or kitchen paper, the bigger the better. Then hear your sounds become louder through them. They may work better if you make two or three holes in the tube. You will actually feel the tube vibrating on your hands as you sing into it.

Where it won't disturb other people, you can use whole rooms and buildings as vibrating resonators. Your singing, as well as your father's when shaving, *does* sound better and clearer in the bathroom, because there is probably less soft furnishing, curtains and carpets in there to deaden sound. If you sing or play an instrument into the corner of the room you can hear the sound better because it bounces back at you.

You will have noticed the sound of aeroplane or car engines bouncing off walls. If you call down empty corridors or into caves, your voice vibrates or even echoes. Underground corridors, multi-storey car parks, archways and bridges, high-walled enclosures, all may reverberate for you if you try them out.

The kazoo in your hand

The kazoo is for you if you cannot afford a real wind instrument. It has been nicknamed the poor man's trumpet, and you can buy one for a small sum of money.

The kazoo is more of an amplifier than an instrument, because it amplifies the sounds you make. So you can hum or sing into your kazoo, and, with practice, make it sound rather like a trumpet, a clarinet or a saxophone. In the early recordings of jazz in the 1920s and 1930s, the kazoo can be heard as an instrument in the old 'jug' bands, often played marching along the streets. (See the 'Listening List', page 62.) What the Americans call 'jugs' would be bottles or jars in England, rather like the old stone ginger beer bottles sometimes seen in junk shops. The easiest equivalent to find today is a large, two-litre wine bottle. The 'umpah' is made by a combination of blowing across the top and singing 'ooh-ooh'. A man's voice is needed to make the deep sounds you hear in jug bands, so you might persuade a father or an older brother to demonstrate for you. Played alongside the jugs and kazoos were washboards (see pages 34–35), fiddles, clarinets – whatever was to hand to make a rousing noise.

You can have a go at singing into an ordinary curved jug to make it resound. Sing 'huh' on one long note, and move the jug slowly over your mouth and chin, and you will hear the tone change and reverberate as you find out the jug's own best note. Lower notes will need your face in a little further, but don't get it stuck.

Jug playing: on the left with an old stone ginger beer bottle, on the right with a large wine bottle

The kazoo was first made in America, round about 1904, being a wooden tube with a hole cut into its wall. Over the wall was a vibrator, made from a stretched membrane. Cheap kazoos use waxed paper for this, but even the cheap ones produce a much better sound than humming through a comb covered with waxed or greaseproof paper, which you can also try.

Today, kazoos are made in metal or plastic. Sometimes a plastic kazoo may vibrate too much. The metal version with a screw top over the vibrator has an advantage. You can take off the top, and check the position of the vibrator. It will sound best if the cardboard ring holding the membrane is placed downwards. Check this, because sometimes the rings are put in upside down. The Concert or Hi-fi kazoo makes a louder noise, because it has an extra horn on top.

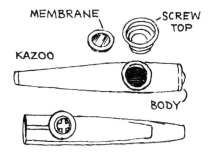

MEMBRANE — SCREW TOP

KAZOO

BODY

Now start singing and humming into your kazoo. The sound changes if you screw the top down, or loosen it. The loose sound is good for open air marching, while the tightened sound is clear, and has less vibrating 'razz'. See for yourself which you like best.

Singing makes more sound than humming, of course, and you can vary the voice you push through the vibrator. Sing up high like a choirboy. Then wail with a wobble, like a rude imitation of an opera singer. If you sing 'liddle-liddle-luddle-luddle' as fast as you can, you will get another interesting sound. Move your tongue inside your mouth, keep your lips still. Or, you can flap free fingers over the vibrator to make your sound fluctuate in a 'wah-wah'.

Sing along through the kazoo with any jazz music you can, to try to imitate the line of, for instance, the clarinet. (See the 'Listening List', page 62.) You will be clever if you can keep in rhythm, but this is something you can experiment with on your own. If you can enlist some friends to join you, a marching kazoo band can try out any tune – pop, classical, jazz, whatever it likes. The American song 'Marching Through Georgia' is an example of an ideal tune for the kazoo band.

3
High and Low: Pitch

You already know that women's voices are higher than men's. Boys' high voices 'break' into deeper voices as they grow up. But have you noticed that we make tunes as we speak in everyday life? We do not speak all on one note; it would sound dull and lifeless, as well as odd, if we did. Try for yourself. Listen hard, and you will hear people raising and lowering the *pitch* of their voices, up and down.

You hear this clearly when phrases are repeated so often they become almost sung: 'All change here.' 'Move right down the bus.' 'Go away!' 'Any old iron?' 'Come and buy my ripe bananas.' In calls and street cries you can hear the tunes which make people listen. You may have heard younger children calling for attention in a sort of song, 'Mummy, Mummeee,' or chanting words to themselves when they are on their own.

Perhaps melody itself came from the way people pitch their voices in daily conversation. In different parts of the world, people's accents make them 'sing' different tunes as they talk the same language. Compare a Cockney accent with Welsh, Yorkshire, Irish, American, and Australian accents when you hear these on radio and television.

If you are learning the descant recorder you will have heard the pitch of the notes you have learnt to sound. Probably you have started with the B above Middle C (on the piano), then one note down to A, then again one note down to G. You might learn a higher note, D above C above Middle C, and gradually be able to play all these notes of different pitch. Each note has its place on the five lines, called a stave, on which they are written.

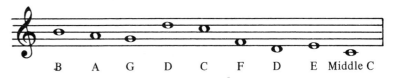

They build up a scale which you can sing, stepping higher in pitch with each note.

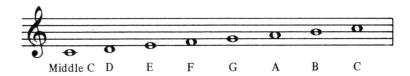

Perhaps you can whistle the scale in tune. It may seem hard to whistle in tune, but try, if you haven't a recorder. Now sing up and up until you can sing no higher and your voice becomes almost a screech. Then sing downwards until it fades out into a growl. You'll have quite a big range from high to low.

What you are able to *hear* in high and low varies from person to person. Some people can hear bats squeak, a note of very high pitch, as they fly out at night. On sunny days, if you have acute hearing, you may hear the shrill whirring of grasshoppers out in an open field.

If your ear is not sensitive enough to 'catch' certain sounds, you may notice that your dog does. His hearing is so acute he may hear higher notes and lower, softer sounds than you. So he will bark at a sound of footsteps before you have heard anything. Dogs also can sing notes. They bark and howl to records and live music, join in with television signature tunes and chiming church bells. Their sense of singing pitch may not be as exact as yours, but it is intriguing to have a pet who sings when you play the recorder, or warbles under the piano stool while you practise.

Again, to demonstrate high and low notes, you can experiment very simply with two pottery pudding bowls and a wooden spoon. Put half a pint of water in one bowl and tap its side. The note it sounds will be of a lower pitch than when you tap the empty bowl.

Tapping while you pour water into the bowl lets you hear the pitch going down

Then try a little water in one bowl and a lot in the other. You can keep changing the notes which sound. And you will soon work out that as the water goes down in the bowl the pitch of the sound goes up. If you can manage to pour water with one hand and tap with the other, you can actually hear the pitch moving. You'll also notice that bowls which look the same may not sound the same, and a cracked bowl will not sound well at all.

A lot of things will make a sound of definite pitch if you strike them, and later on you will be able to put this to the test when making your own musical instruments. Strings stretched tightly can become sounding strings. Metal can also sound notes and so can wood. (See pages 31 and 32.)

Prove this by putting some offcuts of wood or even firewood sticks on a piece of foam plastic, or perhaps a foam bath mat. Tap each stick in the middle with a wooden spoon or pencil. You may find that a shallow flat piece sounds a deeper note than a stubbier thick piece. Hard and soft woods vary in how they vibrate, but usually the longer the piece is, the lower sound it will make. Knots in wood often deaden the sound, so there is a clonk, not a musical noise.

Experiment by working out which beater brings out the best note, and where exactly is the best place to tap. You may find a 'dead' spot which doesn't sound at all. Does it make a difference if you tap with a metal spoon; and does the long handle of your wooden spoon itself sound a note when tapped? It probably does.

To produce a musical sound you have to set something vibrating. If it vibrates *fast*, the pitch will be *high*. If it vibrates *slowly* the pitch will be *low*. The number of vibrations per second is called a note's 'frequency'.

The more you work out ideas with instruments, home-made or otherwise, the better you will be able to hear the difference in pitch between sounds.

Singing

Singing will also improve your ability to hear high and low, and to 'pitch' your own voice.

The human voice is divided into four main groups, according to the pitch which is most comfortably sung. The highest female voice is the soprano. A woman who sings lower notes with more ease is called a contralto, or sometimes alto. The higher man's voice is a tenor and the lower voice a bass.

You may not think of yourself as a singer, but nearly everyone can sing a little, and by joining in with other people you can share the power and pleasure of the sound you all make together. There are many song collections for singing in chorus: action songs, dancing songs, those sung in parts, and rounds. (See the 'Listening List', page 62.)

Probably the simplest round to try is 'Three Blind Mice'. One voice starts singing the rhyme. When this person has sung the first phrase, 'Three blind mice', twice, another joins in, starting at the beginning of the rhyme. Again, a third voice joins, and they all blend together. You feel very clever hanging on to your part till the last voice finishes off triumphantly on its own, 'Three blind mice'.

If you and two friends can manage this, branch out to harder rounds, or try it on recorders as well.

Three blind mice, three blind mice,
see how they run, see how they
run; They all ran aft - er the
farm - er's wife, Who cut off their tails with a
carv - ing knife, Did you ev - er see such a
thing in your life, As three blind mice.

* * *

You can sing to yourself and improve a mood or let off steam. And you can sing along with your favourite pop singer of the moment, so you don't have to be in a group or choir. When you sing a lot you may understand why birds seem to enjoy perching on high trees, trilling and chirping for all the world to hear.

4

Rhythm

excellent if you knock on it with your knuckles, holding one side. Find which makes the best drum, or use them all, each in turn. They will make a good crisp sound for marking a beat.

Rhythm is like the heartbeat of music. When music has a good rhythm it seems to come to life. A conductor will lead singers and orchestras by 'showing' the beat with his hands or a baton. You can have rhythm without pitch or tune; for instance, the beating of a drum to send soldiers marching into battle. The drum is an ancient rhythm instrument, used in warfare, in magic, for sending messages, and for pleasure.

Try drumming on your thighs as you sit on a chair. The next simplest drum you can make to demonstrate rhythm uses any vibrating box. Turn a plastic bucket upside down. Tap the base with a wooden spoon. It may sound louder than if you strike the side. Try out a washing-up bowl upside down, on its base and on its sides. You can also beat at a cardboard box, or a wooden box with one side or its top open. A square two-litre thin plastic ice-cream box is

First try a simple pattern on your drum, counting for each tap:

One, two, three, four,
One, two, three, four . . .

beating steadily.

If you want to go twice as fast, say and beat:

One and two and three and four and
One and two and three and four and . . .

For twice as slow say and beat:

One hold, two hold, three hold, four hold,
One hold, two hold, three hold, four hold . . .

and keep your hand still on 'hold'.

Marching to your drum's beat

Try out these marching ideas with friends, or, if you're on your own, you can count out beats, or use a record (see the 'Listening List', page 62), or the radio, or even tape your own drumming, then march away. Drummers should keep a steady beat for marching in time. The marchers need not go far if you have not much room.

First, march in step to the beat.

Now march on every other beat, so you are moving in slow motion.

Stand still for eight beats, then march again. (It's harder if you count inside yourself than if you count out loud.)

Clap as you march for eight beats.

Next hold a salute as you march for eight beats.

Swing arms in time as you march.

March in one-step squares.

Bend your knees at every fourth beat, for four times.

Try other variations on marching.

Dancing to music

The American song,

> *'I got rhythm,*
> *You got rhythm,*
> *Who can ask for anything more?'*

suggests rightly that it is a gift to have a good sense of rhythm. But you can practise to improve your rhythm. You may feel the beat physically when you hear music and want to join in. Then you can keep time by stamping or clapping, carried along by the strong beat.

Some dancers accent the beat by making extra sounds. Spanish dancers click together little wooden castanets. Tap dancers click

Castanets

with the steel tips on their shoes. Indian dancers sometimes have strings of bells around their ankles or just below their knees, and so do Morris dancers. Some Indian dancers will wear bells round their wrists too, or sewn on to clothing. You can try this out with small metal bells bought from Indian shops or toy shops.

Spanish, Indian, tap and Morris dancers

By dancing to music, even swaying as you try out a guitar, you are singing with your body in time to the beat. The most exciting dancing to watch is when a dancer seems to act out the music by his or her rhythmic movement. Look at a ballet dancer, or see people rocking away to the heavy beat of pop music. Notice the grace of ice-skating to music.

Three dance rhythms

The waltz

(See the 'Listening List', page 62.)

Perhaps you can already waltz. If not, it's easy to learn. Step out with one foot forward, next foot to the side, then feet together. The basic beat is 'one, two three', with the first beat having the strongest accent. Repeat this step in time to the music, twirling round when you come to a corner of the room. The 'old-fashioned' waltz is a quick three, and the modern waltz is taken more slowly.

You can beat it out:

One two three   one two three . . .

and say:

Um-pa-pa   Um-pa-pa . . .

which is written in notes as:

The tango

(See the 'Listening List', page 62.)
This dance is like the Spanish *Habanera* dance, and came to our ballrooms from America, which borrowed it from Africa. Composers have used the tango in songs and other pieces because it has a striking rhythm, with the contrasts of long and short notes.

Say as you beat this typical pattern for a tango:

Lah-di-da-da   Lah-di-da-da . . .

It is written in notes as:

You will notice that the first beat is strongest; and it is a long one.

The calypso

(See the 'Listening List', page 62.)
This is a West Indian dance rhythm, often used in songs, which has attractively contrasting long and short notes. The tune is 'syncopated', that is, a weak beat has an accent, instead of the expected strong one. Sometimes a strong beat is held on, not played, and this

gives a pretty lilt. So, though there are four beats in each group or bar, you may find them divided in this way. The basic beat chugs along as an accompaniment like this:

Um-ja – ja, um-ja – ja, um-ja/   Um-ja – ja, um-ja – ja, um-ja

which is written in notes:

This is not the normal grouping for quavers in $\frac{4}{4}$ time, but is how you would see a calypso written down. Notice the rhythm in this snatch of a song, with its long and short sounds:

Yell-ow bird up high in ban-a-na tree . . .

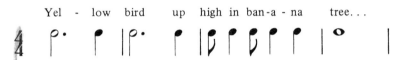

You will hear syncopation in the steady beat of ragtime, and in jazz.

Other dances with interesting rhythms to hear are the rumba, the quickstep and the foxtrot, the samba and the cha-cha-cha.

Dancing rattle dolls

If you do not reckon you are a wonderful dancer yourself, you can always experiment with rhythms you like by jigging an old teddy up and down. Or you can use peg rattle dolls, which are fun to make, and would please younger brothers and sisters as well. Take old-fashioned wooden clothes pegs, and paint them or glue on bits of material for clothes and faces. Painted hair is better than wool or string, because the 'rattle' is a button, fixed on to the flat peg top by a small nail or tack, and wool would deaden the sound. Accept help for tapping with a hammer through the button hole. Leave enough room on the nail for the button to rattle as you walk or dance the doll to music. String or elastic fixed to the nail above the button will give you something to hold and control the doll with.

You would have even more to manage if you could use a puppet on strings to practise dancing.

Processions to the rhythm of music

If a fair or a pageant has a procession it always goes much better with music. It doesn't matter whether this is provided by a smart military band led by a drum major, with booming brass instruments, or a jazz band sitting on an open lorry, with saxophones, clarinets, trumpets and cornets blending together and accenting the off-beat as the musicians are carried down the street. The music sounds exciting in the open air. And it gives the walkers encouragement with a beat to help them along.

Some processions to try out to music

You can hold outdoor processions yourself. You don't even need to have many instruments either. Accompanying, or miming to, recorded music works very well. Of course, it helps to dress up, but what is most important is to work to the music. Use drum beats or other instruments, or recorded music. (See the 'Listening List', page 62.)

A circus procession

You can invent funny walks to music, and be clowns. Also turn cartwheels or make your way on your hands, if you can. At least, if you fall over, you can pretend it is deliberate, because clowns do a lot of tumbling.

Imitate a juggler, throwing balls in time to the music. Hold up two fingers, and juggle with two pretend balls. Then try three. Tilt back your head to watch the circling balls. Catch them and send them spinning round again as you walk steadily.

Or you can pretend to be a trick cyclist on a small-wheeled bike, pedalling along and tipping your bike on to one wheel, concentrating all the time on balance. Sometimes you may roll along 'with no hands, arms outstretched'. Perhaps you had better not fall off!

A procession of footballers

As a loud tune is played you can run out proudly, imagining you are leading your team on to the field. At the end of the game you can display the cup as you walk round the field. Then you can march off even more proudly, as winners.

A procession of athletes

Mime competitors parading round a giant stadium, or mime long-distance runners.

A procession of musicians

Think of a walking band, and, in time to the music, each person can mime playing an instrument. One can beat a drum, slung round his neck. Another can play the flute, held sideways. If you play the trombone you will draw the looped slide in and out as you blow. The trumpeter will toot and move his fingers on the little keys. Playing the violin, the player will draw the bow across the strings with his right hand and hold the instrument in his left hand. Not all instruments can be played as you walk along in procession, but you can add to these.

An animal procession

Any processions to music are good practice for keeping time. Perhaps the most famous procession was of the animals going in to the Ark 'two by two'. You really need a friend for this to make a pair, but you two can keep changing which animals you are. Or make a long list of animal couples, if there are a lot of you joining Mr and Mrs Noah to shelter from the Flood.

On their way in to the Ark:

Mr and Mrs Dog bark and stop to beg for a beat or two.

Mr and Mrs Bear waddle along then stop to hug one another for a beat or two.

Mr and Mrs Lion roar and claw the air.

Mr and Mrs Kangaroo hop and hold their front paws curled up limply.

Mr and Mrs Gorilla beat their chests and lope along.

Mr and Mrs Fish 'swim' along the floor, popping their mouths in time.

Mr and Mrs Crocodile slither along the floor and snap their teeth in time.

Mr Bull snorts and paws the ground while Mrs Cow moos gently and swings her tail in time.

Mr and Mrs Rabbit bunny-hop and munch along, in time if they can.

Mr and Mrs Horse gallop, neigh and toss their heads in time.

Mr and Mrs Elephant lumber along and swing their trunks in time. (Use your right arm for a trunk.)

There are many more animals who can join your musical procession into the Ark.

If you like you can move along to a beat and chant the following song as a chorus. Do your animal actions in time to the music.

The Animals' Song

We must go in to the Ark
Before the rain comes down.
There's space inside for all of us,
No animal need drown.

Noah wants us all inside the Ark
Before the rain comes down.
We'll run and jump out of the Flood
No animal need drown.

A work-out with words

(See also Musical Games, page 46.)

If you listen carefully you will notice that words have their own rhythm. So you can practise playing in rhythm by sounding out words with hands or instruments. The more people who are trying together, the harder it will be to keep in time. If you have enough people, one of you can take a turn to conduct, or point to the words.

Hoping that it does not make you too hungry, think about the names of sweets.

Mars is one beat, written

Humbug is two even beats, written

Chocolate is three beats.
Two short beats and one long, written

Now collect and write a list of sweets on a large sheet of paper or a board. If you know how to write down the notes you can put them underneath. It will be easier if you count four first, before you start the chant, to get everyone ready to come in together. At the beginning clap and say the words at the same time. Then try clapping or beating the rhythm without saying the words out loud, just kept in time by the conductor. If you can do this, you are reading rhythm.

Here are some lists to try, and you can make up your own too.

Twix	Cream Egg	Mars	Marathon
Caramel	Mint	Polo	Chew
Toffee	Sherbet Dip	Bounty	Gum

Next, try these lists of clothes:

Shorts	Sweater	Football boots	Belt
Miniskirt	Track-suit	Woolly tights	Socks
Shirt	Trousers	Sandals	Coat

The rhythm of musical instruments seems to come out even in their names:

Saxophone		Tambourine	Drum
Violin	Cello	Piano	Harp
Glockenspiel	Flute	Recorder	Guitar

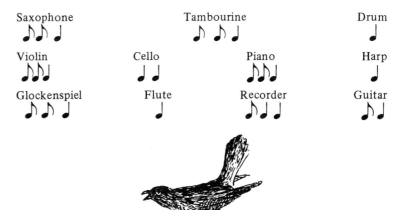

Listen when you can to birds' song. Do they sing in rhythm? Countless composers have tried to imitate their music. (See the 'Listening List', p. 62.) Only the cuckoo's song is an easy one to play with our musical instruments.

Cuck - oo

5

Making Instruments

Home-made instruments use all sorts of odds and ends to make musical sounds, so, as you find out what is useful, it is worth starting a collection. For example, it may be a good idea to eat a lot of ice lollies and to keep the sticks. And ask for any cast-off guitar strings to be kept for you. Some home-made instruments will be imitating real ones.

As you try out suggestions in this book, you will find that you can make your own versions and become an inventor yourself, once you understand how things work. If you can have help with cutting wood or metal and with hammering, you will be able to try out more ambitious ideas. As you become clever at making instruments, you will be able to try more complicated ones. Be curious, and look at any instruments you can, to see what they are made of and how they are played.

Keyboard instruments

Have a look at a piano. It is a keyboard instrument, with black and white keys pressed down by the fingers. If you can have the front part taken off, you will see rows of metal strings, wound round metal pegs, inside the piano. When a key is pressed down, a small wooden hammer covered with felt taps one of the strings, which sounds a note.

The strings are of different thicknesses, and sometimes overstrung, crossing each other to fit in longer strings, and allow for them all to be stretched very tightly. The frame is of iron or steel, which will not buckle or break from the tight tension of thc strings. The sound-

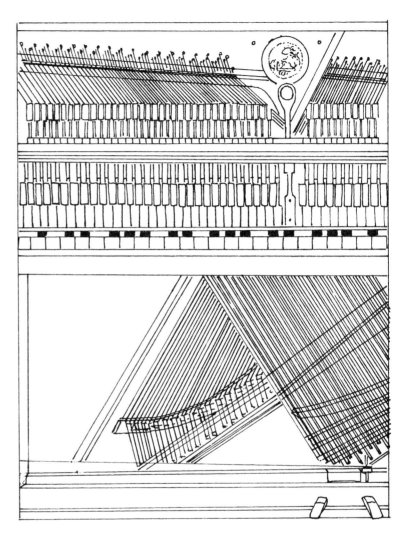

Inside an upright piano. The metal strings stretch almost from the floor, going behind the keys, and then around the metal pegs. Also you can see the felt-tipped hammers which tap the strings when a note is played.

board, which amplifies or enlarges the sound, lies behind the strings in an upright piano and underneath them in a grand piano.

It is worth watching a piano tuner at work if you ever have the chance. The 'action', or works, inside is complicated, but you might well be able to understand it if you saw it happening.

In some keyboard instruments, harpsichord, virginal and spinet, the strings inside are not struck, but are *plucked* by a quill or plectrum. This makes a sound you will recognize as different from the piano. Listen out for it on the radio. (See the 'Listening List', page 62.)

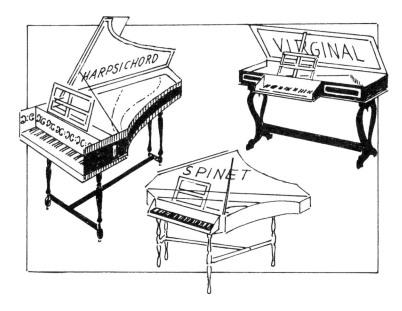

Finger piano

It would be very hard to make a home-made piano, but you can try out a simple finger piano. The 'keys' of your piano are wooden tongue depressors, used by doctors when you say 'ah' for them to look at your throat, and by artists for mixing paints. They are about 15 centimetres long. They can be bought in chemists or art and craft shops. Wooden lolly sticks can be used and will produce good notes too. Plastic garden seed markers are a second best choice after wooden sticks.

Place these spatulas on the table, each with a different length hanging over, separated from its neighbour. Try this out with eight, and have the one furthest to the right with the smallest section overhanging. Put a piece of wood, about 25 centimetres long, on top of the spatulas, and then fix it in place with a C clamp set in the middle of the eight spatulas. The clamp must hold down the wood very tightly. If you use a longer piece than this, try a clamp at each end of the wood, to keep the spatulas rigid.

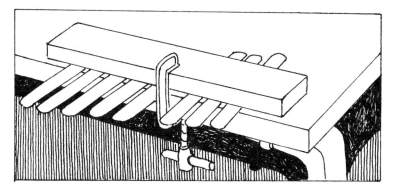

A finger piano

Now, if you stroke the end of each spatula, it will make a satisfying wooden twang. And you will not be surprised to find that the shortest key plays the highest note. This, of course, is based on the same idea as flicking a ruler to make a sound. (See page 11.)

You can play with both hands if you like, or set up several pianos round the table for you and your friends to play together. It is possible to 'tune' these keys to a scale, if you move them carefully, without making a lot of difference between their lengths.

Stringed instruments

Some stringed instruments are played by being rubbed with a bow, or occasionally plucked with the fingers. The violin family includes the slightly larger viola, then the cello, and, with the deepest voice, the double-bass.

A home-made bow

If you want to try bowing a tightened string, experiment with a bow made from a thin, pliable piece of bamboo, about 70 centimetres long. Bend the bamboo, then tie nylon fishing line straight across, as tightly as you can, with good knots. Rubbing resin on the string will help it to slide better when you start using your bow to make a sound with an instrument, like the bucket bass (pages 27–28).

A home-made bow

Plucking stringed instruments

One well-known stringed instrument is the guitar, which is plucked with the fingers or a shaped piece of plastic called a plectrum.

A plectrum

A one-string guitar

You will need some help with sawing and hammering to make this instrument.

Take a piece of wood about 60 centimetres long and roughly 5 centimetres wide by 2½ centimetres deep. Saw two shallow grooves about 8 centimetres from each end of the wood. Into each groove slide a spatula or lolly stick on its side, so that it juts above the wood. These are the two bridges to hold up the string, so that it can vibrate. Use nylon fishing line or nylon string.

Mark the right place, then make a hole about 5 centimetres from each end, so that you can put in a screw-eye to hold the string. This can be done with a bradawl, or you can tap the hole with a hammer and nail to prepare for the screw-eye to go into your wood easily. Tie the string to each end of the screw-eyes, then tighten it by turning it round one of the screw-eyes with a nail pushed through.

To play the guitar, pluck at the string with a finger. If you press the string down on to the wood and shorten the vibrating length, you will of course change the note it makes. If you rest your guitar on an empty box or on a table it will sound louder.

Matchbox harp

Perhaps the easiest and simplest version to make is with a big matchbox without its sliding cover. Find four or five elastic bands of different thicknesses. Then make little notches at each end of the box with a penknife or sharp scissors. Stretch the bands over the box and into the notches. Pluck at your strings with a finger nail or a used wooden match.

Breakfast banjo

Make a plucked instrument by cutting an oval hole in the side of a breakfast cereal box. Or you can use a tissue box. Then stretch elastic or big rubber bands over the length of the box and across the hole.

Pluck them and they will twang for you.

Bucket bass

The original idea of this instrument came from the African earth bow. This was a shallow hole dug near to a young tree. The hole was covered by an animal skin. Then a long string or sinew was stretched tightly from the skin to a high branch of the tree. Pulling at the string while the sapling's trunk bent made it like a big bow. As it was plucked the sound vibrated within the hole.

American slaves adapted this idea by rigging up a plucking bass instrument for homemade bands, using a galvanized steel washtub for the resonator.

In your version you can use a plastic bucket. (A 5-litre paint tin would do as well.) You also need a piece of dowel about 1 metre long and at least 3 centimetres in diameter, and a small piece of wood or a wooden peg. For the plucking string, nylon or gardening twine will do well.

Ask for help to have a hole drilled about 3 centimetres from the end of the dowel. Then ask for a notch to be cut at the other end, so that it can hook over the rim of the bucket, turned upside down. A hole also needs to be drilled in the bucket's base.

Next, tie the string securely on to the wooden peg and thread it through the hole in the bottom of the bucket, from the inside to the outside. Pull your string up, and now thread it through the hole in the stick, which you fix on to the bucket's rim. The stick should be upright from the bucket.

To keep the bucket from skidding, put one foot on the base, opposite the stick. Then pull the stick towards you to brace the string, and try some plucking. It may be hard on your fingers, and

From the top left: a one-string guitar, a matchbox harp, a breakfast banjo, a bucket bass, and the inside of a bucket bass

you may even need a glove for your plucking hand. But you should be able to produce a 'boing' sound.

It might help to put a little piece of notched wood under one side of the bucket, to allow more sound to emerge, if you want more!

Wind instruments

Brass instruments

One group of wind instruments is called brass and includes all types of horns, the cornet, the bugle, the tuba, the euphonium, the trumpet and the trombone. You will recognize them from military bands, seen on state occasions, and perhaps Salvation Army bands too. Basically these instruments are mouthpieces attached to metal tubes. The sound is made by vibrating the lips, forcing air through them, a bit like a controlled raspberry, to set the column of air in the instrument vibrating in its turn.

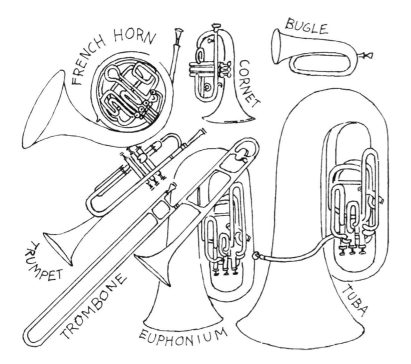

Woodwind instruments

Woodwind instruments have this name because originally they were made of wood, but now they are made of metal and plastic as well and include the recorder family, the flute, the oboe, the clarinet, the bassoon and the saxophone.

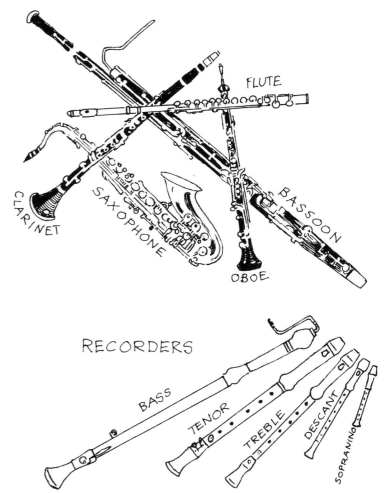

Some woodwind instruments have reeds attached to their mouth-pieces. You can copy this effect by blowing through the metal strip round a cellophane cassette cover or a cigarette packet, or a broad blade of grass, held upright between your thumbs. The grass can produce quite a shriek. A narrow strip of Sellotape folded over once will also sound out like a vibrating reed in this way.

Straw oboe

You only need drinking straws and sharp scissors for this. Paper straws may be easier to make work, but plastic ones wear well and do not become soggy.

Cut a straw into a point, about a centimetre from its end. This then makes a simple double reed. You can see a real one attached to the mouthpiece of an oboe. To make the double reed vibrate and sound a note is a knack.

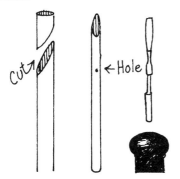

A straw cut into a point; pierced with a hole; an oboe mouthpiece and reed; the top of an oboe

First of all, remind yourself that very little breath is needed. Then put the straw into your mouth and press gently with your lips above the cut reed section. Puff a little air through. The reed must be free to vibrate. Once you can make a sound, it will suddenly seem easy! Keep at it, but do not blow hard.

When you have a note, you can experiment further. Cut off part of the straw, and you will play a higher note. You will find that you can play with a tiny piece. Perhaps this is the smallest musical instrument in the world.

Next make a little hole in the straw. Play the straw oboe, and cover and uncover the hole with a finger, to change the note, just as recorder players do.

The sound your straw oboe can make is an odd one, which has been compared with a bagpipe and even, in one family's experiments, with the mating cry of a tortoise.

Amplified oboe

The sound from a straw oboe can be made louder by connecting it to a rubber or plastic tube, joined to a plastic funnel. The straw can be put into a rubber tap connector if the tube is bent first. Otherwise, to prevent the straw falling right in, it can be held within the tube, with the fingers blocking the rest of the outlet. Then the sound will go out of the funnel and not escape.

If a long tube is used, a deep sound will emerge.

Rubber trumpet

In fact, these parts of a rubber shower attachment can be used with a funnel to make several versions of a homemade trumpet. It works in the same way that brass ones do.

Take one of the rubber tap connectors and fix it on to a plastic funnel. The connector at the other end of the rubber tube will act as your mouthpiece.

Now there is another knack to be mastered. The pressure of air is made quite differently from blowing through a reed. You blow into the rubber tap adaptor like a raspberry done with closed lips; or blowing out as if you were very hot. When you triumphantly make a note, you will find your lips tingling. Producing this noise is the basic technique of sounding a trumpet.

Next you can try out the effect of bending a short tube, say 22 centimetres in length, as you play a note. The bent tube will produce a higher note. With a long tube you can, of course, produce lower notes. Also you can, like a real trumpeter, change the note by the pressure of your lips. Tighter lips produce a higher sound: looser lips a lower sound. The lower sounds the instrument can make may remind you of a foghorn.

You can carry this mouthpiece around and play a length of garden hose, and even play through a plastic watering can if you wish. Perhaps, after all the experimental sounds they have had to bear, your family will be delighted if you *do* take some of your musical instruments out of the house for a while.

Percussion instruments

These instruments are struck, like drums, xylophones, gongs and chimes. They are the easiest to copy with home-made versions of your own. And you may have met some as toys when you were very young, or taken part in a percussion band, beating out the rhythm. You would have used instruments without pitch, as it is enough to keep in time with a drum when you are four or five.

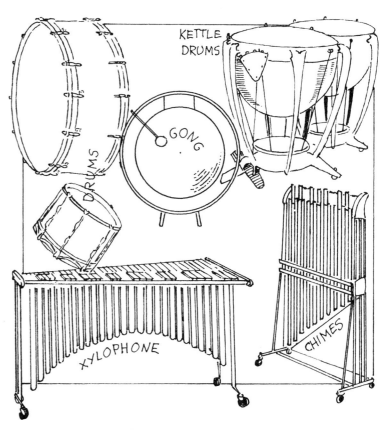

More complicated percussion instruments are 'pitched' so they can produce different notes. For instance, the large drums played in orchestras, the timpani, have skins stretched over them which can

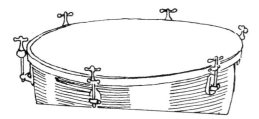

Timpani or kettledrum

be tightened by screws. The note played by the drummer is changed according to how slack or taut the skin is.

Also you may know from school the tuned wooden bars called xylophones. You may have played the single-note metal chime bars, or the glockenspiel. This set of tuned metal bars is also played with hammers. The bars are horizontal, but look out for a different version in a military band. This is held upright, in a wooden frame, shaped like a lyre.

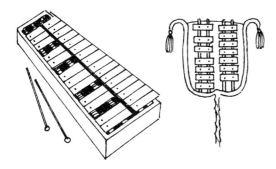

On the left, a standard glockenspiel; on the right, a portable glockenspiel or bell lyre

As you assemble your home-made percussion instruments you find the beater used has a distinct effect on the sound made.

Start looking for beaters in the kitchen. Wooden spoons are excellent, and so are metal ones. Borrow a wire whisk, and a bottle brush too. A pencil with a rubber on its end is also useful. A piece of polystyrene, a cork or a cotton reel, fixed on to a rod of thin dowel,

works well. So does dowel by itself, as a plain drumstick. Long nails can be metal beaters. For a soft end to a stick, wind knitting wool into a ball round the end and secure it with masking tape.

String xylophone

A three-note version is illustrated on page 32, but, if you have the wood and the patience, you can make a larger instrument. You will need pieces of soft wood which are wide and shallow, and say about 35, 30 and 25 centimetres long. Mark and fix screw-eyes (see page 26) about 8 centimetres from each end of the longest piece, 7 centimetres from the ends of the middle piece and 5 centimetres from the ends of the shortest piece. Staples, tapped into the marked place with a hammer, can be used instead of screw-eyes, if you wish.

Use a thick soft string to loop through the screw eyes and twist it to hold the bars apart from each other and to meet in a loop for holding up the xylophone. Each bar will sound a different note. If you can plane or saw wood, or have help to do so, you can tune the bars by taking off small amounts of wood and building up a scale. The xylophone will sound well if tapped with a plastic pen, a pencil or a spoon.

Wood chimes

Cut different lengths of dowel and fix into each one a screw-eye or a cup hook, making a little hole first, as before (see page 26). Thread string through each hook so that the chime can hang freely to vibrate. A row can be hung from nails on a board of wood, or threaded through holes made in the wood. A broom handle could have these chimes tied on to it.

If the lengths are cut carefully, you can tune a set of chimes. Cutting them down a little or sandpapering will change the tone each one sounds when struck with a beater.

Flowerpot chimes

Earthenware flowerpots sound just like bells when they are struck, if they can vibrate freely. So they need to be hung up, on a strong string threaded through the hole in each pot, and held safely by a 'knot', made by a chunk of wood or a bunch of spatulas tied to the string inside the pot.

The pots can hang down from a broomstick, to be tapped with a pencil or wooden spoon. Remember that they are fragile, so they must not be hit hard or knock against each other. If cracked, they will not make good chimes, so inspect them carefully if you buy new ones.

Metal chimes

First find out for yourself how well nails chime by tying a loop of string round 15 centimetre 'wires' or 'cuts', as the nails are called. Tap them with another smaller nail and they really ring.

You can mount a set of swinging nails by tying them on to a small embroidery hoop or a ring of plastic-covered wire. Then make a hanger with strings from the hoop to a curtain ring. The nails can be tapped and also allowed to jingle against each other.

These are some metal chimes you can find at home. Wall brackets can be hung up on strings and struck. Heavy metal coat hangers will chime, so will odd scraps of metal hung up, such as spanners and off-cuts of metal central heating pipes. You can attach the string with masking tape, or have help in having holes cut in the tubes,

near the top, which will not spoil their vibrations. Strike them near the top as they hang, and compare the sounds made by wooden and metal beaters.

If you can have holes drilled for you in empty cans they will sound out good notes when strung up; for instance, between two chairs. You can use fizzy drink cans, food cans with their labels taken off, and larger cans, for a variety of notes. One end of each can should be taken off with a can opener.

You may have heard West Indian steel bands. They use large metal drums, which originally were instruments home-made from petrol drums. (See the 'Listening List', page 62.)

If you or someone else can hit nails straight, you will find that nails driven into a block of wood will sound different notes, according to how much of the nail is vibrating.

Triangle

Again, if you can have expert help in bending aluminium tubing, as in an old television antenna, you can make a triangle like the one shown in the illustration. Of course, it must be hung by a string, to be free to vibrate and tinkle for you. Try a pencil as a beater.

Finger cymbals

More hammering, which may require some help, is needed for these. Take four metal bottle caps and flatten them by hammering. Then hammer a hole in the centre of each one, using a nail. Tap the hole's edges smooth with the hammer. Then put the caps on an old piece of wood, which may get dented. Whack at the holes until you have a hollow around each, to shape your cymbal. Then thread an elastic band through the hole of each cap and loop the band to fit round your thumb, then round your middle finger. Tie little knots to stop the elastic coming out of the holes. When the bands are fixed, put on the cymbals, a pair on each hand, and click them against each other.

Tiny pairs of cymbals were used by dancers as long ago as the time of the ancient Egyptians. And today you may see Spanish dancers accompanying themselves by clicking with castanets, little wooden clackers held in the hand (see page 19.)

Glass chimes

The first thing to remember is that you must be careful how you treat glass; never handle it roughly, to risk cuts.

Bottles do chime like bells when struck with wooden spoons or pencils. You can string different sizes up by their necks to be tapped.

Or you can experiment with playing notes of different pitches by filling bottles with water. Take seven glass one-pint milk bottles and tune them by filling them with different amounts of water, say rising up to two-thirds full to make a scale of notes. Jam jars will also do. To play the octave note, eight above your lowest, you will probably need a larger jar, such as one for fruit juice. If tapped with the edge of a metal coin, the bottles and jar ring out a hard sound. You can play two notes together to enrich your chime. And, if you put the bottles in a close row, but not touching each other, you can make a sliding of 'glissando' of notes, wiping the back of a wooden spoon from one to the next on the fattest parts of the bottles. (See illustration on page 34.)

Drums

You have already seen (page 18) that many boxes will drum well. Metal cans with plastic lids make good drums, each end sounding different when struck.

If you want to make your own drums, you can use either rubber from the inner tubes of cars or lorries or garden plastic sheeting 0.25 millimetres thick. The plastic from record sleeves will work too. First try a simple version with a flowerpot. Cut out a head big enough to cover the pot and go over its ridge. Then tie the rubber or plastic on tightly below the ridge. You can also try out a large pudding or mixing basin, as if you were covering a steamed pudding.

All sorts of cans will make good frames for two-headed drums. Remove the top and bottom of each can with a can opener and press down any sharp edges with a round file. Take great care not to cut yourself. To make a head, cut out a circle of rubber or plastic about 5 centimetres larger than the can's size. Then mark at even intervals, with chalk or felt tip, the places to make holes with punch pliers. These could be about 4 centimetres apart, but you may need some help and advice to decide, according to the size of the can. Strengthen the holes with cloth washers if you can, so they do not tear. When you have prepared two heads, thread string, leather thonging or rubber boot laces through the holes of each circle. Then join one head to the other, stretched down the can. Criss-cross through the threading, as in the illustration on the next page. When you can get the heads tightly stretched, they make a good sound.

Scraping

Although scrapers and rasps often make noises rather than beautiful sounds, they can have a place as musical instruments because they give an edge to the rhythmic beat of percussion. You may have heard them, for instance, in Latin American dance music.

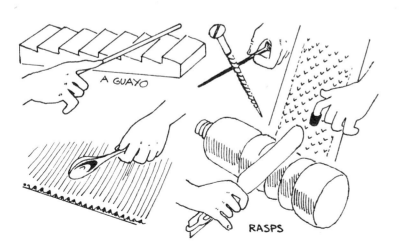

One kind of scraper is a notched stick rubbed up and down by a smooth stick. The Indian version is called a *guayo*. To make a proper one you need the help of a carpenter, to cut teeth into a piece of wood for you.

You can try for yourself the effect of scraping a nail up and down the turns of a large screw. Or rub an old metal thimble on a metal grater, or a metal spoon on corrugated cardboard, or a spatula on ridged plastic bottles and containers.

Sound blocks

You will need some small blocks of a soft wood like pine, and sheets of various grades of sandpaper or emery paper. Cut a piece of sandpaper to fit over one side of a block with some overlap. Use this to wrap over the sides, then fasten down the sandpaper with drawing pins. Glue a cotton reel on to the uncovered side, to use as a handle.

Try out the different grades of roughness of sandpaper, because they will make varying sounds as you brush your sand blocks gently backwards and forwards against each other, one in each hand.

Washboard

Home-made bands, like 'jug' bands and skiffle bands, have found the old-fashioned metal or thick ridged glass washboard, still seen in junk shops, a useful rhythm instrument. Jazz and blues musicians have used it too.

If you manage to find a washboard you play it like this. Hold the wooden frame in your left hand and use the right hand to sound it, with metal thimbles on your fingers and thumbs. Or you can have thimbles on the three largest fingers of each hand and the thumb. Hold the board upright and scrape up and down the corrugated zinc, which makes two different sounds. Or tap it like a snapping or snare drum. You can try wedging the washboard between your knees to free your hands, but it must be rigid.

Sometimes players have hung contraptions on to their washboards, like pots and pans, bells, even cheese graters, to act as chimes. But probably you will have your hands full trying to drum a washboard.

A washboard, with extras and without

Shaking

You knew about one kind of shaker when you were a baby, and that was a rattle. It is a firm container with a filling which makes a pleasant noise when shaken about. South American maracas are the musical instruments based on this idea, and originally they were made of dried gourds. You may have some plastic or wooden maracas at school. They are not only shaken, but tapped against the free hand, or they can make a trembling sound when circled in the air.

A home-made maraca

This can be made with a tin can which has a plastic lid. First fix a piece of dowel, longer than the tin, under the middle of the plastic lid, with a washer and a woodscrew. Ask for help to make a hole in the bottom of the tin, so that the dowel can be pressed through it and jut out, to make a handle. Put some pebbles or dried peas into the tin, then push the dowel right down until the plastic lid can fit over the top. Tape it round the edge, to keep the tin shut tight.

Other rattles

Even simpler rattles can be made with small metal tins or wooden, cardboard or firm plastic boxes with lids, filled with rice, beads, small nails or big seeds. Tape the lids on, so that you can shake them without losing the fillings.

Bamboo shaker

A thick hollow piece of bamboo can be closed with a cork and glue or tape after you have put some rice into it. Then you will have a delicate shaker as the rice grains roll inside.

If you ever have a chance to look at American Indian instruments, you will see that their dance rattles are made of wood, turtle shells, sea shells, gourds and other natural materials. The shakers you make will also go well with dancing.

Bag shaker

A softer, rustling sound will come from shaking clean foil milk bottle tops in a big plastic freezer bag, tied at the top. You need to collect a lot of tops, though they must have room to move about in the bag.

Shakers on strings

These can be made with buttons, keys and metal curtain rings.

Water shaker

Quite a different sort of shaker can be made by shaking a marble gently in a closed jam jar, half full of water. It really clonks and gurgles.

Tambourines

Perhaps you once played a tambourine in a percussion band. One home-made version of a tambourine is made by punching holes about 7 centimetres apart near the edge of a tin foil plate, or three paper plates glued together. Then prepare jingles by hammering holes in the middle of crown bottle tops with a nail, having first removed any cork lining. If the edges of the holes are rough you can smooth them with coarse sandpaper or a round file. Then thread the tops in pairs, back to back, on split curtain rings. Fix one ring with its jingles through each hole on the plate. Then your tambourine is ready to shake.

Another way to make a tambourine is to thread bottle tops back to back on a ring of wire. Make a handle by binding the place where the wire is joined with tape or a piece of cloth.

Jingling Johnnie

Prepare more bottle tops, say about twenty-five or thirty. With help, hammer a hole in the middle of each top. Then press a nail through each hole and fix this jingle on to a pole or broom stick. Use round headed nails for this, and hammer them in so that they are secure, but have space for the tops to shake up and down on the nails. Also leave some of the stick bare so you can hold your instrument.

The Jingling Johnnie beats time. To make sure that you hear the jingles rather than the pole thumping on the floor, fasten a rubber door stopper on to the foot of the stick. Or a large cork glued on would soften the thud just as well.

Watch instruments being played live or on television. A cellist does not seem to *rub* his bow on the strings so much as stroke them carefully. You will see that the drummer does not need to wallop his drum to get a good note. He gives it a controlled tap. Players draw the sound out of their instruments by their skill in handling them, and so can you.

Another place to see instruments is in a museum, where they are often on show as beautiful objects. Sometimes recordings of their sounds are provided as well. Also look out for any local craftsmen, or people at exhibitions and festivals, who make and repair instruments. Some may be making copies of old instruments such as lutes and harpsichords, assembling them by hand. When you know that a violin has over seventy parts, you realize how skilled the person is who puts the instrument together. It is worth asking to visit him in his workshop.

The more you know about how musical sounds are made, the easier it will be to make instruments and to change them to suit your own needs and ideas.

6

Noise Makers and Sound Effects

Brothers and sisters who have put up with your experiments may consider that most of the home-made instruments make a noise rather than musical sounds. And you can admit that many of the following suggestions really make noises. Some, though, are attractive to hear as well as fun to play. And some will be useful for sound effects in plays when 'musical' timing is essential. Also you may need sound effects for 'noises off' in any mini-operas or songs you might attempt (see pages 52–61.)

Sounds you can make

Sound effects can start with you and your voice. Some are just a special way of talking. With your speaking voice you can shout, shriek and whisper.

Different ways of just breathing make sounds: you can sigh, gulp, gasp, swallow, blow, pant, gurgle, cough, sniff, sneeze, snore and snort. If upset, you can groan, cry or sob. If pleased, you might laugh, chuckle, giggle, whistle, hum and sing.

Simple sound effects

These suggestions can be altered and added to, but give you an idea of the huge number of sounds you can easily make. They can be made into a guessing game, if you like, with the sounds made out of view. Or you can challenge a friend to work through the whole list at top speed.

Tinkle: with a spoon and a drinking glass.
Drip: with a tap into a bowl of water.
Squeak: by stroking a balloon.
Bounce: with a ball on a hard surface.
Knock: with knuckles on a door.
Clap: with your hands.
Pop: with a plastic beaker upside down on a bowl of water, lifting it suddenly into the air.
Crackle: by screwing up stiff paper.
Roll: with a rolling pin on a table or draining board.
Shuffle: with your shoes on a hard floor.
Skid: with a bare foot on a wet surface; but take care not to fall.
Slam: a door.
Tear: sheets of newspaper.
Scratch: with your fingernails on any hard surface.
Pound: with clenched fists on a table or on the floor.

You can make a huge collection of effects. It would be useful to decide what makes a satisfying sound, and practise it, because later on you may want to produce it to order.

A noisy poem

You might like to try saying this verse either on your own or in chorus with friends, practising supplying the supermarket sound effects bang on time! If you can make your sound effects so that they fit into the rhythm of the verse, it will work much better.

Supermarket Song

When we go down to our supermarket,
'Specially on Saturday,
It's the noisiest place I've ever heard;
We can hardly hear what we say.

There are people who clump up and down,
Looking at prices with a frown (clump, clump).
They pick up baskets with a clank (clank, clank).
And talk and choose and take and thank.

They roll out trolleys with a squeak (squeak, squeak).
That one's needed oiling for a week.
Some tins are knocked down with a crash (crash).
And when it's bottles, what a smash (smash).

We push our trolleys round the shop,
When we've all we want at last we stop.
We'll pay for our shopping now, I think.
The money rattles with a chink (chink, chink).
The cash till drawer has got a bell,
Ping ping it goes, and slam as well (ping ping, slam).
People keep coming in and out.
To speak over the noises you've got to shout (a chorus
    of noises all together, as many as you can manage).

When we get home we've forgotten the tea-bags,
We're hungry and it's time for tea;
So we're glad to run round to the shop at the corner
Then make in peace a cup of tea (teacups clatter).

Imitating real sounds

Working with these effects, you have to concentrate to produce the noise at the right moment. Otherwise you might have a pistol shot when it should be pouring rain.

Rain

This sound can be made with a wooden rain box. You might be glad of some help. The box needs to be long and narrow, say about 1 metre long by about 15 centimetres high and 15 centimetres wide. Ten-centimetre nails should be hammered into the base, so that they stick up inside the box. Put a handful or so of whole dried peas into the box and fasten on its lid. Hold the box and tip it up and down. The speed of the peas running from one end to the other can give the idea of a slow trickle or a heavy downpour. Or you can hang the box up from a screw-eye attached to a rope in the centre of the lid, and tip it like a see-saw to make the rain sound.

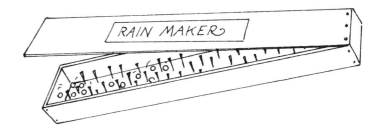

Sea sound

Some whole dried peas rolled steadily round and round in a wire sieve give an impression of the sea surf breaking on the shore.

Thunder

Hang up a large sheet of thin metal and shake it from one corner. You will need to have holes to thread the string. One big shake followed by gentle ones will give the effect of a peal of thunder and its echoes. A large tin tray is a fairly good second best, if you tap it on your knee to vibrate.

Water running over pebbles

This effect can be copied by quick and gentle tapping up and down a wooden xylophone. (See page 31.)

Rowing in a boat

The sound can be suggested by swishing the beaters up and down a wooden xylophone. (See page 31.)

Marching feet

These can be imitated by even strokes on the sound blocks. (See page 34.) Then try marching fast, or slowly for a funeral procession.

Shots

Strike a padded chair or stool, best made of leather or plastic, with a thin garden cane, which will make a cracking sound.

Breaking glass

Prepare, with great care against cuts, some odd bits of broken china, and collect them in a bucket. Then empty them into a second bucket. You can do it slowly or quickly, and vary the amount of pieces. Metal buckets will make more din.

Horses' hooves

You can clap half coconut shells against each other, holding them cupped in your hands. Or you may find it easier to clonk them rhythmically on bricks, stone or tarmac, to imitate a road. Practise the horse cantering in the distance, then galloping close, and off away again, the sound growing fainter. Or your horse can stamp on the ground, and you can provide the snorts and neighs yourself.

Some more noise makers

Look round the kitchen again. You can make a gong by striking a frying pan or a large saucepan lid with a wooden spoon. Hang them up or hold the handles, so that the main section can vibrate.

Cups tied on to a rope, then tapped, make a pretty chime. Foil plates will sound if struck, and tin trays are well worth beating for sound.

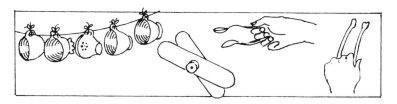

Cups tied on a rope; date box clackers; playing the spoons; clacking pork rib bones

The wooden tops and bottoms of date boxes make clackers when struck together. You can glue cotton reels on to them to make them easier to clash against each other.

'Playing the spoons' used to be an old music hall turn, and they are still heard in folk and dance music. Tea spoons may be easier to use if you have small hands, in case larger ones cause blisters. Wooden salad spoons click well, but perhaps the best sound comes from round stainless steel soup spoons. The art of a spoonist is quite complicated, but you can try out the clicking by holding the spoons back to back in your right hand, clicking them against each other. You can sit down and tap them against your other hand or against your leg.

You can tape the handles with sticky tape to stop them skidding in your fingers. They may click better if bent a little at the neck, so you had better use old ones.

Dried pork rib bones also make good clickers if you clonk them against each other.

Blowing bubbles with a straw in a jug or a bottle makes a satisfying gurgle.

Wind chimes

You can let the wind do the work for you to make noises. Wind chimes can be made from many different materials, like the other sorts of chimes. (See page 32.) This time, you can hang them up from a triangular frame, made from three pieces of wood nailed together. Or, for light chimes, a cheese box lid with holes punched into it will do as a holder. The idea is to mount the chimes close together, so that they jangle against each other when they move. They are set moving by being hung in a draught, say over a doorway, or from the branch of a tree. Or you can blow them or give them a touch to start them swinging and playing.

Good wind chimes can be made from nails and other pieces of metal, strips of wood and dowel, or bamboo. They need not be of the same size.

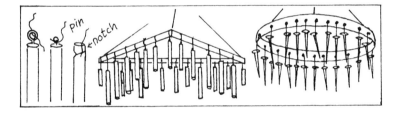

Wind chimes

In Shakespeare's play *The Tempest*, Caliban talks of his island being 'full of noises, Sounds and sweet airs, that give delight and hurt not'. That island was enchanted, and perhaps you have not yet made 'a thousand twangling instruments' like those which hummed round Caliban's ears. But your music making will begin to give you delight and in time will please other people too.

7

Making Up Music

By now you may have put together some home-made musical instruments. Also you may own or be able to borrow some real instruments. If you can join in a group with a few interested friends, you can take another step forward. When you play with other people, you are trying out a very important part of making music. There are new things to do.

Not only will you play your own part in a group, but you will have to listen very hard to the other players. This has been compared with having a 'third ear', which you can use for hearing what the others are doing. First of all you have to make sure that your part fits in, that you keep in time with the others. And you must not play so loudly that you cannot hear them. Neither must you play so softly that they cannot hear you. You will all depend on each other.

Perhaps it would be easier to take turns to 'conduct'. Then the players can all watch the conductor, who will point at who is to play, and stop and start the playing, rather like a policeman on traffic duty. He or she can beat time for you too. Just keep the signs you agree on simple, as you experiment in making up music.

Talk with your instruments

This is a good way of beginning. Let one player play a little tune of two or three notes. Then another player can answer him or her, either copying the sound, or making up something different. Contrast different sorts of sounds: high and low in pitch; beaten or blown. There is endless variety at your fingertips.

A short snippet of rhythm can be copied in the same way, if your instruments are unpitched. Try it slowly, then quickly; loudly, then softly.

The conductor can add to this, if there are enough people, by a solo player 'speaking', then a group of players answering. Next, they can all play together, and have a tiny idea of what a concerto for a soloist with an orchestra is like. (See the 'Listening List', page 62.)

Sound pictures

You can talk together about building up pictures with sounds. Using your instruments or sound makers, work out how to give an impression in music of, for example, a storm. Make up and use sound effects. (See pages 38–41.)

A storm

Start with a rumble of thunder. Then have some pattering rain. The thunder grows louder; drums might help the claps of thunder. The rain becomes heavy. Then the conductor begins to quieten the piece down, and the noise becomes less. The thunder dies to a rumble, and the rain drizzles into silence.

You can try these ideas too, then make up subjects of your own.

Outer space

Echoes will be good for a space theme, and so will any high-pitched or strange sounds. The impression should be unearthly, so weird sounds will be excellent. They do not have to be beautiful, and perhaps you should try to make them very different from the 'real' music we already know. A fade-away ending would work well.

Water scene

You could be at the sea-side, by a river, or lake. The idea is to imitate the sounds of water moving: splashing, gurgling, running, flooding. Try bubbling straws in water. Glass chimes might work well too, but you must decide what to have.

A working machine

Bring out clickers and clackers, and work on interweaving rhythms. Sharp tapping and beating will be effective. The conductor will need to keep all the parts of the machine in time, unless, of course, it breaks down, is mended and starts up again. That would be a test of the players watching the conductor.

Ghosts

Here you have scope for mysterious sounds. Perhaps you can set the scene of your sound picture by chiming twelve o'clock for midnight, when the ghosts dance out of the misty darkness. Trembling notes, nothing too loud or too definite, will seem scary. Let your sounds shimmer together.

Musical moods for one

If you are on your own and want to try making up music, you can experiment with moods. First you might listen to some music. (See the 'Listening List', page 62.)

Then try making up tunes or rhythms which match a mood.

Lively: Play in quick notes, mixing long and short ones. Perhaps pluck at strings.

Angry: Play little bursts of sound: beating in sharp rhythms would show the mood. Beat two instruments at a time, and let the sounds clash together.

Restful: Play slow quiet notes on an instrument which makes smooth sounds.

*   *   *

Once you start making up your own music, you realize how clever the composers are who write for large choirs and orchestras, and all kinds of instruments. But their works do not just arrive. The composers have tried out many new ideas. They have been explorers in sound. And so can you be, in a small way.

It may be that you are pleased with what you or your group have managed to play, and yet do not know how to write it down. This can be done.

43

Your own musical language: noting down

Long before you are able to 'read music' you can make musical signs. If you work with a partner or in a group you can note down sounds in your own musical shorthand. This can then be a record of anything you make up, to add to or change as you wish, and to use next time.

First try with your singing voice only, to 'ooh'.

● can mean a short note, and ▬ a long one.

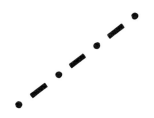

This would mean a short note followed by a long one, in a pattern, rising in pitch (getting higher).

The note might waver about.

It might waver up,

or down.

It might move straight up,

or down.

It might move into a circle.

It can sing out in whirls, like the wind howling.

It could swoop up, or shoot down.

Your voice could sing 'uh' sharply, six times, which might be written:

To keep voices together, one singer can point through the signs. For a big group they could be drawn with thick felt-tip on a large sheet of paper, or chalked on a board. Your voices may hum smoothly up and down.

The sound can die away.

Other sounds can be added: Try saying 'sh' with clenched teeth, first pushing the lips forward then smiling.

sh   >   <   >   <   >

The mouth can make popping noises, opening and shutting with tight lips.

pop — — — — — —

Obviously, fatter signs should be sung louder:

soft   loud   soft   loud

Smaller zigzags could mean faster

slowly   fast

Try a horse clopping in your throat, or saying 'k' at the back of your throat. Make up signs for these and any other sounds you can create.

8

Musical Games

Test your ears

You will need: a chair, a blindfold and different instruments or noise-makers. (See pages 38–41 for ideas.)

Every player except one has an instrument. They make a circle round a blindfolded boy or girl, who sits on a chair in the middle. Taking turns, a person plays his instrument. When the blindfolded person guesses correctly what is being played, he gives up his chair to that player. The blindfolded listener can also try to place the player, and see if he can hear where the sound comes from, pointing the direction.

Another version of this game is to collect instruments, show them and sound them to all the players. Then everybody except one leaves the room, with the door a little ajar. The player in the room sounds an instrument. When somebody outside guesses what it is, he can come in, and make a sound, until everyone has guessed correctly.

Or you can score points, with the player inside changing instruments. He wins points for the number of noises he has to make before the correct answer is given.

Hunting high and low

Go round the house, collecting things which can make a tone or sound, say by tapping. This may be easiest in the kitchen, though you must take care of china or glass. Have a competition to see who finds the highest note, or the lowest, in a given time.

Rhythm guessing

Each player has a drum or other percussion instrument, which can be home-made. The players sit in a circle. The first player taps out a name and gives the letter it begins with. For this game you can use first names, place names, the names of foods, or what you like. The player who guesses correctly is the next to make a rhythm.

Can you guess the tune?

This game is played by one person thinking of a tune or song, and singing the first or last section, or a few bars.

The other players guess what the tune or song is, and the winner has the next turn.

Musical memory

Decide on an order, or you can play this game round a circle. The first player sings a note, then the second sings the first note and adds one of her own. Each player then in turn adds to the tune, just as long as the singers can keep up composing and remembering.

Singing tongue twister

Another version of the game above is to make up a singing tongue twister, which might build up something like this:

Ma
Mata
Mata
Matahigh
Matahigh
Matahighlow
Matahighlow
Matahighlowpiggle
Matahighlowpiggle
Matahighlowpigglebin
Matahighlowpigglebin   and so on . . .

The first person to stumble can start a new pattern, and you may produce some marvellous nonsense singing.

Humming forfeits

You need a hat, with slips of paper on which forfeits are written out. The forfeits are to do with music, like clapping a tune or answering a question about instruments.

Someone in the circle of players hums a tune to another player. If he can't guess what it is, he does a forfeit, taking a slip from the hat. And if he can't manage the forfeit, he is out of the game.

Guessing an instrument

Write the names of musical instruments on slips of paper. Each player has a slip pinned to his back, without seeing the name. Then each person in turn asks the other players questions, to find out what his instrument is. They can only answer 'yes' or 'no'.

When a player has found out his instrument, another slip is put on his back. The person who collects most slips is the winner.

Musical miming

Cards with pictures of musical instruments on them must be prepared, and one put into an envelope for each new turn.

Players sit in a circle, and a card is passed round in the envelope, while music plays. When the music stops the player holding the envelope takes out a card and mimes playing the instrument on the picture. The others have to guess what it is. Anyone who guesses wrongly is out. The last person in is the winner.

Musical quiz in a bag

This needs some questions and answers on all kinds of music prepared by someone who is not in the game. Questions about music are written on slips and put in a bag. An adult keeps the answers in a list and sets music playing while the bag is passed round a circle. When the music stops, a slip is taken out and read aloud.

If that player answers correctly she wins a point. If not, someone else can try for the point. When the bag is empty the player with most points has won.

Music-man's buff

This game works out well with nine players, but can be played with less. Eight players choose a note each, going up the scale from low 'doh' to high 'doh'. Each one sings his or her note and the ninth person tries to remember who has which note. You can sing the name of the note or not as you wish. Then he is blindfolded, and chases round, trying to catch someone. When he does so, he has to decide whose voice it is from the note the person sings. If he is right that person is blindfolded, and the blindman is out.

Or, if you prefer, the blindman can take on the note of the person he catches as *his* note, but this might be hard to manage.

Musical snap

Make a set of cards, drawing musical signs, notes or instruments, with two of each kind. About fifty cards would be good, but it depends on how much you know or can find out from looking at printed music or books.

Shuffle and deal out the cards evenly among the players. Each player puts her pile face down. Then at the same moment all the players turn over their top cards. If two cards are the same 'snap' is shouted. The first person to shout wins the cards on show. The winner is the one who gains the whole pack.

To make this game hard, people who can read music can try singing any notes on the matching cards, checking their attempts with an instrument, before winning the cards.

Skipping to music

I like coffee, I like tea,
I like you, so skip with me!

You can play skipping to music outside, singing the rhymes in time to the skipping, with people skipping in and out of a big turning rope.

Or, if you have space, you can try skipping inside with your own rope in time to a record or tape. The music needs a strong beat, and it's good practice in trying to keep time.

If you are a clever catcher, you can try throwing or bouncing and catching a ball to music, which is tricky. Even more ambitious is to try to swim to music.

Singing circles

Draw on large sheets of paper or mark out six circles, and put in each one a piece of paper with the name of a song or nursery rhyme on it. Spread them round the room. Then shake a dice and jump into the circle which has that number. If you can't sing the song written on the piece of paper in that circle you are out, and the next player takes a turn. As the songs or rhymes are sung, replace them with new ones.

Notes and clefs

On big cards write some notes and clefs. Pin them up round the room or hall.

Music is played and children dance to it. When the music stops the organizer calls out, for example: 'Run to treble clef.' Those who run to the right place are in. Others are out, and the game goes on till a winner is left.

Musical corners

This game is similar to 'Notes and clefs'. It needs some preparation, but is good for a lot of players. An organizer has a list of tunes and their first notes, copies of their titles, and four helpers.

The players stand in the middle of the room and hear the first part of a tune played or sung. (This can be done backwards, if you want to make the game very hard.) The helpers in the corners hold up tune names, and the players go to the corner with what they hope is the correct name. Those who are wrong are out.

Musical jigsaw

If you can read music, you can copy out a short tune, like part of a nursery rhyme, then mount it on thin card. Cut this into uneven pieces, then see if you can fit your own jigsaw together to make a tune again.

This could also be done with a picture of an instrument, copied or traced from a book, mounted and made into a jigsaw.

Mixed-up songs

You will need a ball and a long list of songs, hymns, carols and nursery rhymes.

Throw the ball round a circle of players. Each person has to clap three times before catching. When someone catches the ball she is given the names of two songs. She has to sing the words of one to the tune of the other, for four marks. If she cannot do that, she can score one mark for singing the tune of each song.

The winner is the one who has most points when all the tunes on the list have been used.

There must be a million more musical games. Why not make up some of your own?

9

Playing with Tapes

If there is a cassette recorder in your house it is probably used to play the family's favourite pop music, and you may dance to it. Or you may do keep-fit exercises to the music. At school, teachers probably use cassettes in many lessons.

If you can have the use of a cassette recorder, there is much more to be done as you try to make music. The cassette recorder can help you to listen, as well as to record.

First, if you talk or sing, then play the recording back, it will sound 'different', because usually you hear yourself mainly through the bones in your head, which relay the sound to your ears. Instead, the sound from the cassette recorder has travelled through the air. Try blocking your ears and singing or talking to yourself, and you will see how this works.

If you sing or play the recorder or another instrument, then play that back, you will hear the music more clearly. Any little mistake or hesitation which you had no time to notice will come out at once. This then is a very good way of spotting mistakes, or noting when you have played too fast or too slow, and what you can try next time to improve your playing. It can be disheartening to hear the 'fluffs' which you had to play through to keep going. If you are patient, though, you can use a taped performance of a piece to help you find the weak parts, before you have a music lesson and your teacher points them out.

Of course, there is a great deal more to record than your own playing, or your performances with friends. You can tape the instant music you make up when improvising. (See pages 42–43.) This will be another record of what you have done, as well as writing it down in signs. (See pages 44–45.) One group can criticize another, and make suggestions for new versions of the music composed. Again, listening to what a group has done, played back on tape, will show you how good the texture of sound is: it may be too full of recorders, or they may be swamped by drum beats. It may be boringly all-the-same loudness. Perhaps the music seems too rushed, so that nothing is clear, and the tape records a muddle of sounds. When you are not actually playing or conducting you will be able to hear much more clearly what can be cut, or repeated, or extended.

Also you can tape ideas of music to keep them safe until you can work them out properly; try them with other instruments or with more people. A short snatch of a tune then will not disappear into thin air.

Taping everyday sounds

Apart from your own music, you can tape everyday sounds and build up a sound collection. Leave about ten seconds blank between each sound. If you list the sounds as you record them, this tape can be used as a quiz, with your friends guessing what each sound is. Also the collection will provide excellent sound effects for productions. Then you can add your home-made sound effects (see pages 38–41), and use both in the mini-opera, (see pages 54–61), or for plays. Putting sounds together in this way is quite near to composing music.

Some sounds to try to record

Water going down the sink.
A splashing tap.

A ball bouncing off a brick wall.

The same ball bouncing off a wooden door.

The same ball bouncing on a tennis racket.
A bee flying from one flower to another.

A car starting.

A train passing.
A dog's bark.
A cat's miaow.

The voices of farmyard animals.
The voices of zoo animals.
Crowd sounds: in the school playground;

in the swimming baths;
in a supermarket;
at the station;
at a fairground.

Birds

Dozens of composers have tried to imitate bird-song, often so beautiful that we are lucky if we hear it every day. (See the 'Listening List', page 62.) You can make a point of listening to birds, trying to record them singing in the rain, in the evening, and, if you can wake up early enough, even their first singing of the day, the 'dawn chorus'. You will soon notice that the amount of singing varies from season to season.

Birds sing long solos, answer each other, show off their voices, and you may catch them imitating your music too. Blackbirds have been known to copy human music. It may not be particularly easy to catch a bird's song unless you are near to it, and other sounds, like aeroplane engines, do not interrupt. Remember that it is not good for your cassette recorder to be kept out in hot sun. You may be glad of help from bird-watchers as you try to track birds in quiet places. It is a triumph when you have managed to record some singing, even if it sounds rather a long way away.

If you do become seriously interested, you may have to try to borrow a directional microphone to help you catch the bird-song. A lot will depend on the quality of the cassette recorder. Also some bird songs are so high we can hardly hear them. But it is a challenge to try to capture that airy sound.

Making up sounds to tape

With a friend, you can play a game in which one tells a story while the other supplies sound effects on the spot, with voice, instruments, or whatever is to hand. Whenever the story teller pauses, a sound has to be provided to illustrate the story. You may find yourselves laughing at your attempts, but try and keep the story going, then laugh when you play it back.

*   *   *

Theatres now use taped sound effects a great deal, and it may help school productions, particularly if you are short of musicians or people, to be able to tape the music and sounds wanted ahead of a performance.

Obviously you will have to practise your own skills at dealing with a cassette recorder, and while you do so, you will find out a lot about sounds.

10

Mini-operas

One of the most exciting musical performances to watch is an opera. It is a drama set to music. You may have seen or even taken part in an opera. Some have been composed specially for children. (See the 'Listening List', page 62.) There can be some spoken dialogue, as in an ordinary play, but in an opera the music has an essential part. It is not just a few songs added to the play. The singers act out a story as they make the music with an orchestra.

Sometimes, instead of speaking the words between the main songs, the characters keep the story going in a speech-like singing. This is called 'recitative'. The words are free in rhythm, and sung as near to talking as possible, as if the characters were having a conversation in song. To give an example of this style, there are two mini-recitatives for you to try out, sung by two characters. (See pages 53–54.) Also you will find a longer mini-opera (see pages 54–61), to give you a flavour of what opera is like.

There are many kinds of songs, or 'arias', which the characters in opera sing to tell their feelings or continue the story. To give you an idea of the different songs there can be, you can work through the list which follows, using it as a guessing game with a friend. Or practise by yourself in front of a mirror.

What am I singing?

You can act these songs out to a record of background music, or you can sing to made-up words or nonsense sounds. The miming will help when you try to act and sing in the opera. (See pages 54–61.)

Pop-song

Hold a microphone and dance with it. Jerk your body in time to the music, and make faces which are full of expression; perhaps of misery, anger or love.

Lullaby

Rock a baby and sing softly.

Sacred song or hymn

Hold a hymn-book with both hands; bow your head sometimes, reverently. The rhythm can be stately.

Military song

March about; stand stiffly to attention; salute.

Sea-song or shanty

Steer a ship; pretend that a ship is rocking under your feet; tug at sail ropes; imitate a horn-pipe.

Comic song

Trip over your own feet; grin and leap about, or fool around, dancing.

Patriotic song

Wave a flag and sing soulfully.

Indian song

Clap your hand over your mouth; whoop; dance an Indian war-dance, creeping then jumping.

Spanish song

Pretend to play a guitar and sing, or dance a twirling dance with castanets clicking in your hands.

Cowboy song

Sit astride a chair as if it were a horse; juggle with the reins and swish a lassoo.

Sad song

Sing slowly with sad gestures, holding your head and weeping. Wipe your eyes with a handkerchief.

Love song

Sing tenderly; smile affectionately. If you like, kneel, as if you were serenading your loved one.

Operatic song, or aria

Sing as if you were performing with a huge orchestra in a grand opera. Open your mouth wide, as if you were 'holding on' to long notes. Make sweeping gestures with your arms. You can 'die' dramatically at the end of the song if you wish.

Sometimes opera singers are teased for spinning out their death scenes. So you can spin yours out a bit too, and perhaps clutch the dagger which stabbed you, as you 'take your time' to die.

Recitative: speak-singing

Try this out with a friend, or on your own, being two characters, which is much harder. Think of yourself as half-singing, and do it in just the same rhythm as you would when speaking. The lines below are printed in groups of words to help you, rather like the bar lines and phrases of written-down music. Try the conversations out, changing over the parts.

*   *   *

Scolding

Mother: I thought I asked you
To clear up your bedroom?

Child: I didn't hear you
And it doesn't need it.

Mother: Need it! The place is in a tip.

Child: I like it that way.
And it *is* my bedroom.

Mother:	It's me who's the one
	Who does all the cleaning.
	So I need that floor cleared.

Child: I'll clean it for you.

Mother: And hoover in the corners?
And throw out all the rubbish?

Child: There isn't any rubbish.
But I will clean up the corners.

Mother: All right. I'll let you have a try.
You are off school today, after all.
I'll come back here in half an hour,
To see what you have done.

Child: What have I let myself in for now?
But at least I can play my radio
While I shove my stuff
Into the cupboard.

*　　*　　*

Wheedling

Child: I've seen some track shoes in the sale.
They're very cheap.

Mother: They need to be.

Child: It says they're half-price.

Mother: Then there's sure to be something wrong with them.
Bought-in rubbish for the sale.

Child: No, it says they're perfect.

Mother: But they may not have your size.

Child: It says all sizes are in stock.

Mother: I suppose you've chosen
The colour you fancy!

Child: The blue and white ones are the best.

Mother: I've a lot to do
Before I can go shopping.

Child: If I give you some help
Can we go this morning?

Mother: I'm not promising, mind you,
Till I have seen them for myself.
Made sure that they are worth the money.

Child: I'm sure they're worth every single penny.

Mother: I can see you soon selling in a market,
Wheedling the people
To buy any old junk.
You could sell ice-cream to Eskimos
The way that you're going.

Child: I'd rather be buying.
Can we set off soon?

*　　*　　*

Now see if you can make up or improvise your own dialogue. Let your partner know when you have finished a speech by a glance. You will find that a lot can be simply questions and answers, which are easy to sing.

You might try *Gossiping*: 'Have you heard . . .?'
or *Hunting*: 'Have you seen my . . .?'

A mini-opera

Witch and wizard spells

Props needed: two metal coal scuttles for cauldrons; a table for them to be placed on for stirring; two outsize wooden spoons; a broomstick; gold wrapping paper; various items of food.
Instruments: whatever you can manage of these: a rattle for the Wizard; guitar; recorder or other pitched instrument; chime bar or home-made chimes.

Music by Glenda Parkinson

*(Enter **Witch**, with cauldron, a coal scuttle, on her back. She props
up her broomstick and sings:)*

Witch

Good morn - ing, Wiz - ard Slum - ber - slow, I see you're up at
last. I thought I'd call to see you As I was fly - ing past.

Wizard

I can't think why you nev - er walk; It's al - ways rush and flur - ry. You'll
nev - er do things well, I say, If you do them in a hur - ry.

55

Witch

When you do an-y-thing well at all, We'll all be flab - ber -

gast. I don't ex-pect you've start-ed To make a real break - fast.

Wizard

How could a flight-y witch like you With the name of Nip-pe-ty Quick, Un-der-

-stand the spells I have in mind As you flit on your lit - tle broom - stick?

Witch *(scornfully, speaking or speak-singing, whichever comes easiest.)*

What are these wonderful spells?

Wizard

More wonderful than you could make.

Witch

I'll believe that when I see them.

Wizard

I never make a mistake.

*(**Witch** puts down cauldron on table, and sings her spell to quick chimes, while stirring.)*

56

Witch

1. All right then, Wiz - ard Slum - ber - slow, I'll put you to the
2. I have my caul - dron on my back, My spell you will ad -

test. We'll try in a com - pe - ti - tion Whose spells can work the best.
mire; As I work out my mag - ic, The piles of food grow higher.

The Spell
Witch

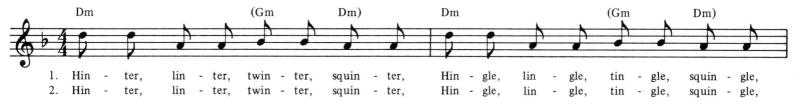

1. Hin - ter, lin - ter, twin - ter, squin - ter, Hin - gle, lin - gle, tin - gle, squin - gle,
2. Hin - ter, lin - ter, twin - ter, squin - ter, Hin - gle, lin - gle, tin - gle, squin - gle,

Here's a spell I am beg - in - ning You will find I can't help win - ning.
Quick as I can eat my din - ner You will find that I'm the win - ner.

(*Witch takes out from the cauldron various pieces of food. Use whatever looks good. The point is that there must be room in the cauldron for two sets of food, one of which is wrapped in gold wrapping paper. She might produce two bananas, a box of cereal, a packet or a roll of biscuits, and a tin of fizzy drink.*)

Witch (*offering a banana, with pride*)
You can eat a little if you like.
I know that you're so slow,
It might take you a fortnight
To bring out such a show.

Wizard (stirring his cauldron with great concentration)

My magic takes a little time.
The food which now you hold
I'll work on with a special spell,
And turn it all to gold.

Witch

You talk of your wonderful spells.

Wizard

More wonderful than you can make.

Witch

I'll believe that when I see them.

Wizard

There will be no mistake.
Pass me the banana, the box of cereals, the biscuits, the fizzy drink.

(She does so, and he puts them all into his cauldron, and starts to sing his spell, in a dreamy chant, to slow chimes.)

The Spell
Wizard

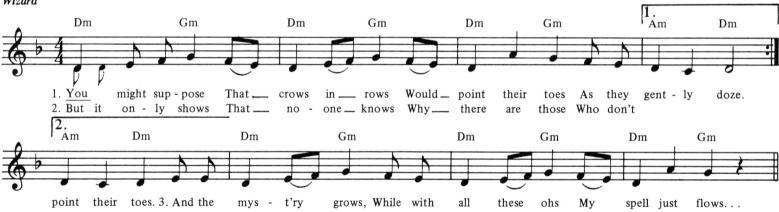

1. You might sup-pose That crows in rows Would point their toes As they gent-ly doze.
2. But it on-ly shows That no-one knows Why there are those Who don't

point their toes. 3. And the mys-t'ry grows, While with all these ohs My spell just flows. . .

(Witch sighs and looks unimpressed until the gold objects are produced.)

Wizard

See. Here you are.
Gold bananas, cereal, biscuits, drink;
How's that for a magic feat?

Witch (still not wanting to be impressed)

It may seem pretty clever to you,
But what are we going to eat?
That was for breakfast,
Not just a spell.
I'm getting hungry.

58

Wizard

Oh very well *(rather crossly).*

Witch

I hope you'll change it back again,
Or I'll turn you into a toad.

Wizard

You'll have to ask me nicely

After the cleverness I showed
You'd better do what you are told.
Or you'll find yourself a witch of gold.
(He shakes his magic rattle threateningly.)
And I'll make you dance at such a pace,
You'll wish we'd never had a race.

Witch *(beginning to sing his spell, mockingly, at the same time holding her nose . . .)*

Witch

Let rows of crows Now point their toes. I'll hold my nose And his spell just grows.

Wizard's rattle: 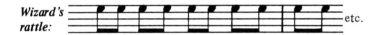 etc.

Wizard *(suddenly warming to her)*
Did I hear you singing my spell?

Witch
Did I hear you playing mine?

Wizard
And did you hear they went together?
The duet sounded fine.

Witch
But that gold food is not for eating;
It doesn't put me in a trance.

I'm feeling like a snack to eat
Not a cosy little dance.

Wizard *(persuading her)*
Witch, if we put our spells together
What magic we might do?
The slow and quick could work great wonders
With fun for me and you.

Witch *(considering)*
I suppose we might try something out;
And we can work out how,
First eat some food that I have made,
Undo your spell for now.

(To quick and slow music or chimes by them or others, they eat some of the uncovered food which he brings out of his cauldron, say a banana each. The chimes beat through a verse of the spells.)

Witch:
(Chime bar - D*)

Wizard:
(Recorder*)
*Or any suitable instrument you have.

Witch

Yes, if I make food and you make gold,
How lucky we will be.
We'll eat and spend together,
Join spells so cleverly.

*(**Witch** and **Wizard** sing together, arm in arm.)*

Witch and Wizard

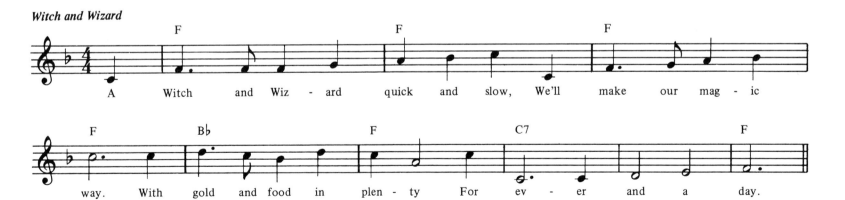

(And they go off together at the end of the verse.)

60

If you like, this version of the last song can be played on instruments
at the end of the mini-opera.

(Chime bars - C*)

(Recorder*)

* Or any suitable instrument you have.

Notes used in 'Witch and Wizard Spells'

CODA, a last note

You may never compose great music, or thrill thousands of people
with your singing. You may never be able to play what you hear so
clearly in your head, as you try out new instruments. But if you start
to make your own music now, it will give you pleasure, and an
interest which will last all your life.

Listening List

Some other music to enjoy

These are some popular works by the composers listed. If you like one piece, listen and look for others by the same composer.

Beatles, The:	*Sergeant Pepper's Lonely Hearts Club Band*
Beethoven:	*Pastoral Symphony*
Bernstein, Leonard:	*West Side Story*
Brahms:	*Clarinet Quintet*
Britten:	*A Young Person's Guide to the Orchestra*
	Saint Nicolas
Chopin:	Mazurkas and polonaises for piano
Copland:	*Rodeo* and *Appalachian Spring*
Delibes:	*Coppélia*
Dukas:	*The Sorcerer's Apprentice*
Dvořák:	*Ninth Symphony, From the New World*
Gershwin:	*Rhapsody in Blue*
Grieg:	*Peer Gynt Suite*
Handel:	*Entry of the Queen of Sheba*
	Water Music
Haydn:	*Toy Symphony*
Humperdinck:	*Hänsel and Gretel*
Joplin, Scott:	Piano rags
Lloyd Webber:	*Joseph and the Amazing Technicolor Dreamcoat*
Mozart:	*Eine Kleine Nachtmusik*
Mendelssohn:	*Fingal's Cave Overture*
Mussorgsky:	*Night on the Bare Mountain*

Prokofiev: *Peter and the Wolf*
Rimsky-Korsakov: *Flight of the Bumble-Bee*
Saint-Saëns: *Carnival of the Animals*
Schubert: *The Trout Quintet*
Strauss, Johann: *Tritsch-tratsch Polka*
Tchaichovsky: *The Nutcracker Suite*
                             The Sleeping Beauty
Vivaldi: *The Four Seasons*
Wagner: *The Ride of the Walküre*

Index